MSUGH TER, M.D

The Shadow's Secret

Copyright © 2024 by Msugh Ter, M.D

All rights reserved. No part of this publication may be reproduced, stored or transmitted in any form or by any means, electronic, mechanical, photocopying, recording, scanning, or otherwise without written permission from the publisher. It is illegal to copy this book, post it to a website, or distribute it by any other means without permission.

This novel is entirely a work of fiction. The names, characters and incidents portrayed in it are the work of the author's imagination. Any resemblance to actual persons, living or dead, events or localities is entirely coincidental.

First edition

*This book was professionally typeset on Reedsy.
Find out more at reedsy.com*

Contents

The Loom of Destiny	1
The Thread of Mystery	5
The Weaving Begins	10
The Hidden Path	15
The Cursed Glade	21
The Sorcerer's Lair	27
The Hidden w	33
The Enchanted Grove	39
The Shadow's Secret	45
The Final Confrontation	52
The Dawn of a New Era	57

The Loom of Destiny

Elara lived in a village where the air always seemed to shimmer with a touch of magic. Her home was a quaint cottage nestled at the edge of the village, surrounded by trees and flowers. The cottage was filled with the warm scent of wool and dye, for Elara was the village's weaver. Her small shop, with its colorful threads and bright tapestries, was a place of comfort and creativity.

Every day, Elara worked at her loom, crafting beautiful pieces of fabric that told stories of the village's past. The people believed that the loom was special, that it had the power to reveal the future. Elara had always known there was something different about her loom. When she worked, she sometimes saw shimmering threads in the air, like tiny ribbons of light. She thought little of it, dismissing it as part of the magic of her craft.

One crisp autumn morning, a strange feeling filled the air. Elara was busy weaving a new tapestry, her fingers moving with practiced ease. She loved the rhythm of the loom, the way the threads danced under her hands. But today, the threads felt different. They seemed to hum with a quiet energy.

As she worked, the doorbell of her shop jingled softly. Elara looked up, expecting to see one of the villagers. Instead, an old woman walked in. Her clothes were old-fashioned, with rich colors and intricate designs that reminded Elara of the tapestries from long ago. Her eyes were sharp and curious, and she had a kind, knowing smile.

"Good morning," Elara said, her voice warm. "How can I help you?"

The old woman nodded politely. "I've come to leave something for you," she said, placing a bundle wrapped in a faded cloth on the counter.

Elara took the bundle, feeling its weight. It was surprisingly heavy for its size. The old woman's eyes twinkled as she spoke again. "This is a gift, but also a task. It holds secrets that need unraveling."

Without another word, the old woman turned and left, her footsteps fading into the distance. Elara unwrapped the bundle, revealing a tapestry. It was different from any she had ever seen. The colors were dark and muted, and the patterns were strange and intricate. There were figures woven into the fabric—people and places Elara did not recognize. The tapestry seemed to glow softly, as if it had its own light.

Elara's curiosity was piqued. She hung the tapestry on the wall and studied it closely. As she looked, she felt a chill run down her spine. The figures on the tapestry moved, almost as if they were alive. The faces seemed to watch her, and the patterns shifted in subtle ways. It was as if the tapestry was telling a story, one that had not yet come to pass.

She decided to work on the tapestry in her spare time. Each day, as she wove and worked, the tapestry seemed to reveal more of its secrets. Elara began to notice that the tapestry depicted events that hadn't happened yet. There were scenes of the village, strange symbols, and even a figure who looked remarkably like herself.

One evening, as Elara was finishing up her work, a young man walked into the shop. He was tall and handsome, with dark hair and a serious expression. He looked around with a sense of purpose, his eyes finally settling on Elara.

"Hello," he said, his voice smooth and deep. "I'm Aiden. I heard about the tapestry you've been working on. I was hoping you could tell me more about it."

Elara was taken aback. "How did you hear about it?" she asked, her curiosity getting the better of her.

Aiden smiled slightly. "I have my sources. I believe the tapestry is important. It's not just a piece of art—it's a map of fate."

Elara's heart skipped a beat. She had never told anyone about the strange feelings she had while working on the tapestry. "What makes you think that?" she asked.

Aiden stepped closer to the tapestry, examining it closely. "I've seen similar tapestries before, in other places. They show the future and guide those who can read them. I think this one is special. It's connected to something important, and I believe we need to understand it."

Elara and Aiden spent hours studying the tapestry together. The more they looked, the more they realized that the scenes depicted were not random. Each figure, each pattern seemed to be part of a larger story. They saw a dark figure standing on the edge of the village, and strange symbols that appeared to be a warning.

As the days passed, Aiden became a frequent visitor to Elara's shop. They worked together, trying to decode the tapestry's secrets. Aiden was knowledgeable about many things, including ancient symbols and old legends. Elara found herself growing closer to him, not just because of their shared quest but because of the way he listened and understood her.

One night, as they were working late, a sudden gust of wind blew through the shop. The lights flickered, and the tapestry seemed to shimmer with a strange light. Elara and Aiden looked at each other, their eyes wide with amazement.

"It's as if the tapestry is reacting to something," Aiden said.

Elara nodded, feeling a sense of urgency. "We need to figure this out quickly. There's something important about to happen."

They continued their work late into the night, piecing together the clues from the tapestry. As they worked, Elara felt a growing sense of unease. The tapestry seemed to be showing a darker side of the village's future, with shadows creeping in and figures being pulled away.

Just as the first light of dawn began to appear, Elara and Aiden made a breakthrough. They discovered that the tapestry was not just a map of future events—it was a warning. There was a powerful force moving towards the village, something that could change everything.

Elara looked at Aiden, her heart pounding. "We need to do something. We need to find out what this force is and how to stop it."

Aiden nodded, determination in his eyes. "We will. Together, we'll uncover the truth and protect the village."

As the sun rose, casting its golden light over the village, Elara and Aiden knew that their journey was just beginning. The tapestry had shown them a glimpse of what was to come, and they were ready to face the challenges ahead. With the loom of destiny guiding them, they set out to uncover the mysteries and protect their home from the darkness that threatened to engulf it.

The path ahead was uncertain, but Elara felt a renewed sense of purpose. With Aiden by her side and the tapestry as their guide, they were ready to face whatever fate had in store for them.

The Thread of Mystery

The morning sun had just started to warm the village when Elara and Aiden gathered in the small room behind Elara's shop. The room was filled with the smell of fresh fabric and the soft clinking of the loom's shuttle. Elara sat at her loom, the strange tapestry hanging nearby. Aiden was pacing, deep in thought.

"We need to understand more about what we're seeing," Aiden said. "The tapestry is important, but we don't know enough about what it's showing us."

Elara nodded. "I agree. It seems to show something dark coming toward the village. We need to figure out what it is before it's too late."

They decided to start by researching old village records. Elara's shop had a small library of ancient books and scrolls. They spent hours sifting through dusty volumes, hoping to find clues that matched the symbols and scenes on the tapestry.

One old book caught their attention. It was a leather-bound journal with a faded cover. Inside were notes about old village legends and historical events. The pages were filled with drawings and writings about magical beings and ancient protectors.

Elara turned a page and gasped. "Look at this! It's a drawing of a dark figure—just like the one on the tapestry!"

Aiden looked over her shoulder. "That's strange. It says here that this figure was a powerful sorcerer who once threatened the village. According to the legend, he was defeated long ago and sealed away."

Elara's eyes widened. "Could it be that the figure on the tapestry is this sorcerer? If so, why is he appearing now?"

Aiden thought for a moment. "It's possible. But we need to find out more about this sorcerer and how he was sealed away. There might be more clues in the village's history."

They decided to visit the village elder, who was known for her knowledge of old stories and traditions. The elder lived in a large, ivy-covered house at the edge of the village. Her garden was filled with herbs and flowers used for healing and rituals.

The elder welcomed them with a warm smile and invited them inside. Her home was cozy, filled with the scent of dried herbs and burning incense. They sat at a wooden table, and Elara and Aiden explained their findings.

The elder listened carefully, nodding as they spoke. "The sorcerer you've read about is indeed a part of our village's history. He was a powerful and dark figure who sought to control the fate of the people. He was defeated by a group of brave villagers who used a powerful spell to seal him away."

Elara leaned forward. "Do you know how the spell was performed? Is there any way to stop him from returning?"

The elder thought for a moment. "The spell was performed using a special crystal, which was said to be the source of the sorcerer's power. The crystal was hidden away in a secret place, guarded by a special group. If the sorcerer is returning, it might mean that the crystal has been found or the spell has been weakened."

Aiden frowned. "Where can we find this crystal? And how can we protect the village?"

The elder looked at them seriously. "The crystal's location was never written down, to keep it safe. However, there are old legends about a hidden chamber in the forest where the crystal might be kept. You will need to find it and ensure the crystal remains safe."

Elara and Aiden thanked the elder and set out to find the hidden chamber. The forest was dense and full of secrets. They walked through the trees, following a path that seemed to twist and turn on its own. The sun filtered through the leaves, casting dappled shadows on the ground.

As they ventured deeper into the forest, they came across strange markings on the trees. They looked like the symbols on the tapestry. Elara and Aiden followed the markings, feeling a sense of both excitement and unease.

After a while, they reached a small clearing with an old, abandoned building in the center. It was covered in vines and looked like it hadn't been used in years. The building was round, with a stone archway leading inside.

"This must be it," Aiden said, examining the archway. "It looks like the entrance to something important."

Elara nodded. "Let's go inside and see what we can find."

They stepped through the archway and into the building. The inside was dark, with only a few rays of light coming through cracks in the walls. The air was musty, and the floor was covered in layers of dust.

They explored the building carefully, looking for clues. In the center of the room was a large stone pedestal with an inscription on it. Elara dusted off the inscription and read it aloud.

"The path to the crystal is hidden by time. Seek the light within the darkness, and the way shall be revealed."

Aiden looked around. "We need to find what this inscription means. There must be something here that will help us."

They searched the room, moving aside old debris and examining every corner. Finally, Aiden noticed a faint glow coming from a crack in the wall. He pressed on the wall, and a section of it slid open, revealing a narrow passage.

Elara and Aiden entered the passage, which led them deeper into the ground. The passage was dimly lit by small, glowing crystals embedded in the walls. They followed the passage until they reached a large underground chamber.

In the center of the chamber was a pedestal, and on it rested a crystal—a large, glowing gem that radiated a soft light. The crystal was beautiful, with colors shifting from blue to green to purple.

"This must be it," Elara said, her eyes wide with awe. "The crystal that holds the sorcerer's power."

Aiden approached the pedestal carefully. "We need to take this back to the village and ensure it's protected. But we must be careful. If the sorcerer is already on his way back, he might try to take the crystal from us."

As they prepared to leave, they heard a noise behind them. They turned to see shadowy figures emerging from the darkness of the chamber. The figures were cloaked and moved silently, their eyes glowing with a sinister light.

Aiden drew his sword, and Elara grabbed a small lantern they had brought with them. "We need to fight our way out of here," Aiden said. "Stay close."

They fought bravely, using their wits and skills to fend off the shadowy figures.

The battle was fierce, but they managed to hold their ground. With a final push, they defeated the figures and made their way back to the passage.

Elara and Aiden emerged from the forest, exhausted but determined. They carried the crystal carefully, knowing it was the key to protecting their village. As they reached the village, the sun was setting, casting a golden light over the peaceful scene.

They rushed to the elder's house, where they explained everything that had happened. The elder was relieved to see the crystal and listened carefully as Elara and Aiden described their encounter with the shadowy figures.

"You've done well to retrieve the crystal," the elder said. "But we must act quickly. The sorcerer's return will bring great danger. We need to strengthen the spell that keeps him sealed away."

Elara and Aiden worked with the elder and the villagers to prepare for the sorcerer's return. They placed the crystal in a safe place and performed rituals to reinforce the protective spell.

As night fell, Elara and Aiden sat together, watching the stars. The village was safe for now, but they knew that the danger was not over. The tapestry had shown them a glimpse of what was to come, and they were ready to face whatever challenges lay ahead.

The path ahead was uncertain, but Elara felt a sense of hope. With Aiden by her side and the village united, they were prepared to confront the darkness and protect their home. The adventure had only just begun, and they were ready to face whatever fate had in store for them.

The Weaving Begins

The next morning, the village seemed unusually quiet. Elara and Aiden had returned late the night before, their hearts heavy with the weight of their task. They had stored the crystal in a secure place within the elder's house, where it would be safe until the spell could be properly reinforced.

Elara woke early, the rays of the sun gently warming her room. She stretched, feeling the tiredness in her bones. There was still so much to do, and the sense of urgency was palpable. She quickly dressed and made her way to her shop, where Aiden was already waiting for her.

"Good morning," Aiden said, his face serious. "We need to start preparing for the next steps. We have to make sure the tapestry and the crystal are protected."

Elara nodded. "I agree. We need to understand the tapestry better. It might give us more clues about what's coming."

They spent the morning studying the tapestry in detail. Elara and Aiden carefully examined each scene, each figure. The tapestry was filled with intricate designs, and the more they studied it, the more they realized how complex it was.

"I noticed something," Aiden said, pointing to a section of the tapestry. "This part shows a group of people standing together, facing a dark force. It looks like they are preparing for something."

Elara squinted at the tapestry. "Yes, I see that too. It seems to suggest that there will be a group of people who will play a role in what's coming. Maybe we need to find and gather these people."

Aiden nodded. "That makes sense. We should talk to the elder again. She might know more about these people or how we can find them."

They hurried to the elder's house, where they found her in her garden, tending to her herbs. She welcomed them inside and listened as they explained their findings.

"The tapestry is showing us that we need to gather allies," Elara said. "Do you know of any people or groups who might help us?"

The elder thought for a moment, her eyes thoughtful. "There are a few ancient families and old groups in the village and the surrounding area who have a history of protecting against dark forces. They might be able to help you."

Elara and Aiden took note of the elder's suggestions. They decided to visit these families and groups to seek their help. The village was surrounded by several smaller hamlets, and they planned to travel to each one.

Their first stop was the Harper family, known for their bravery and skill in combat. The Harper family lived in a large farmhouse on the edge of the village. When Elara and Aiden arrived, they were greeted by the head of the family, a tall, strong man named Thomas Harper.

Thomas listened carefully as Elara and Aiden explained their situation. "The dark forces you're talking about are serious," he said. "We've had our share of battles in the past. If you need help, we'll stand with you."

Thomas agreed to help and offered to gather his family members to join them in their quest. Elara and Aiden thanked him and moved on to the next family, the Silvers, who were known for their knowledge of ancient magic.

The Silvers lived in a quaint house surrounded by a beautiful garden. When they arrived, they were welcomed by Martha Silver, an elderly woman with a kind face. Martha listened intently and agreed to help, offering her knowledge of old spells and charms.

"The magic in this village runs deep," Martha said. "I'll do what I can to help protect the village and strengthen the spell."

With the help of the Harpers and the Silvers, Elara and Aiden continued their search for other allies. They visited the Greens, a family of skilled trackers, and the Rivers, who were known for their wisdom and insight. Each group agreed to help in their own way, providing skills, knowledge, and support.

As they worked to gather their allies, Elara and Aiden also prepared for the next stage of their plan. They needed to perform a ritual to reinforce the protective spell around the crystal. The ritual required special ingredients, which Elara and Aiden gathered from the forest and the surrounding areas.

One evening, as they were preparing for the ritual, Aiden looked at Elara. "We've done a lot, but I feel like there's still something missing. Do you think we have everything we need?"

Elara thought for a moment. "We've gathered allies and collected the ingredients. We've done everything we can. We just need to trust in the process and hope that it's enough."

The night of the ritual arrived. The village was filled with a sense of anticipation as everyone gathered at the elder's house. The crystal was placed on a pedestal in the center of the room, and the villagers stood around it, ready to perform the ritual.

The elder led the ceremony, guiding everyone through the steps of the ritual. The air was filled with the scent of burning herbs and the sound of chanting voices. Elara and Aiden stood beside the pedestal, their hearts pounding with a mix of hope and anxiety.

As the ritual continued, the crystal began to glow brighter, its light spreading through the room. The villagers chanted in unison, their voices rising and falling in a rhythmic pattern. The energy in the room grew stronger, and Elara felt a sense of warmth and protection.

Suddenly, a gust of wind swept through the room, causing the flames of the candles to flicker. The light from the crystal grew even brighter, and the shadows in the room seemed to come alive. Elara and Aiden exchanged worried glances.

"We need to stay focused," Aiden said, his voice firm. "The ritual must be completed."

The elder continued to lead the ceremony, her voice steady and commanding. The villagers followed her lead, their voices blending together in a powerful chorus. The light from the crystal intensified, and the shadows seemed to recede.

As the ritual came to an end, the light from the crystal began to fade. The room grew quiet, and the villagers looked relieved. The elder smiled at Elara and Aiden. "The spell is now reinforced. The crystal's power is protected."

Elara and Aiden thanked the villagers for their help and went outside to take a breath of fresh air. The night was clear, and the stars shone brightly overhead.

"We did it," Elara said, her voice filled with relief. "The crystal is safe, and the spell is stronger."

Aiden nodded. "Yes, but we can't let our guard down. The sorcerer may still be out there, trying to find a way to break free."

They walked through the village, talking about their next steps. They needed to stay vigilant and continue to protect the village from any threats. The tapestry had shown them that there were challenges ahead, and they were ready to face them.

As they returned to their respective homes, Elara felt a sense of hope and determination. With Aiden by her side and the support of their allies, she felt confident that they could face whatever came their way.

The adventure was far from over, and there were still many mysteries to uncover. But Elara knew that they were not alone. With the strength of their allies and the power of the crystal, they were prepared to confront the darkness and protect their home.

The night was calm, but the journey ahead would be filled with challenges. Elara and Aiden were ready to face whatever fate had in store for them. Together, they would unravel the mysteries and safeguard their village from the dark forces that threatened to engulf it.

The Hidden Path

The days after the ritual were filled with a sense of cautious calm. The village had settled back into its usual routine, but Elara and Aiden knew that they couldn't relax just yet. The dark force still loomed, and the sorcerer's return was a threat that could not be ignored.

One morning, as Elara and Aiden walked through the village, they noticed something unusual. The forest, which had always been a place of peace, seemed darker and more foreboding. The trees appeared thicker, their branches twisted like skeletal fingers.

"Do you see that?" Elara asked, pointing to the forest edge. "It looks different."

Aiden squinted into the shadows of the trees. "Yes, it does. It's as if something is changing in there."

They decided to investigate. The forest was dense and the path was narrow, but they pushed through the underbrush, moving carefully. The air was cooler and the forest seemed eerily silent.

As they ventured deeper, they came across a small, hidden clearing. In the center of the clearing was an old stone archway, covered in vines. The archway seemed ancient, and it looked like it hadn't been touched for a long time.

"This looks like it might be important," Aiden said, examining the archway.

"It's not on any map I've seen."

Elara nodded. "We should see where it leads."

They stepped through the archway and found themselves in a narrow tunnel. The tunnel was dark and damp, with only a few small, glowing crystals in the walls providing light. They walked cautiously, the sound of their footsteps echoing softly.

The tunnel twisted and turned, leading them deeper underground. The air grew cooler, and the smell of damp earth filled their noses. After a while, they reached a large, underground chamber.

The chamber was filled with old relics and ancient symbols. In the center of the room was a large, stone pedestal with a strange, glowing map laid out on it. The map was covered in symbols and lines, and it seemed to be moving slightly, as if alive.

"This map must be important," Elara said, her eyes wide with curiosity. "It might show us something we need to know."

Aiden examined the map closely. "It looks like it's showing different locations. Maybe it's pointing us to something."

They studied the map carefully, trying to understand its meaning. The symbols on the map matched some of the symbols they had seen on the tapestry and in the old books. The map seemed to highlight a few specific locations, each marked with a different symbol.

"We need to visit these places," Aiden said. "They might hold the answers we're looking for."

They marked the locations on their map and prepared to leave the chamber.

As they turned to go, they heard a noise behind them. They spun around, their hearts racing. Shadowy figures began to emerge from the darkness, their eyes glowing with an eerie light.

"We're not alone," Elara said, her voice trembling. "We need to get out of here."

Aiden drew his sword and stood ready to defend them. The shadowy figures moved closer, their forms shifting and changing. Elara grabbed a small vial of glowing liquid from her bag and threw it at the figures. The liquid burst into a bright light, pushing the shadows back.

The figures hesitated, their forms flickering as if they were struggling against the light. Elara and Aiden took their chance and ran toward the tunnel. They hurried through the twisting passage, their breaths coming in quick gasps.

As they emerged from the forest, they looked back to see the shadowy figures fading into the darkness. They were safe for now, but the encounter had left them shaken.

"We need to be more careful," Aiden said, his voice firm. "There's something dangerous in that forest."

Elara nodded. "We have to focus on the map. It's our best chance to find out what's coming."

They spent the next few days preparing for their journey. The locations marked on the map were spread out, and they needed to plan their route carefully. They packed supplies and gathered information about each location.

Their first destination was an old, abandoned tower located on a hill outside the village. The tower was said to be a place of ancient magic, and it was one of the locations highlighted on the map.

Elara and Aiden set out early in the morning, following a winding path up the hill. The tower came into view as they climbed, its tall, crumbling walls standing against the sky.

When they reached the base of the tower, they found an old wooden door, barely hanging on its hinges. Elara pushed the door open, and they stepped inside.

The interior of the tower was dusty and filled with cobwebs. Sunlight streamed through broken windows, casting eerie shadows on the walls. They carefully made their way up a spiral staircase, which creaked under their weight.

At the top of the tower, they found a small room with an old, wooden table. On the table was a dusty book, bound in leather. Elara picked up the book and blew off the dust, revealing an intricate design on the cover.

"This looks like it might be important," Elara said. She opened the book and began to read.

The book was filled with writings about ancient spells and magical artifacts. It mentioned a powerful artifact known as the "Heart of Light," which was said to have the ability to protect against dark forces. The Heart of Light was described as a gem that radiated pure light and was hidden in a secret location.

"This is exactly what we need," Aiden said. "If we can find the Heart of Light, it might help us protect the village."

The book provided clues about the location of the Heart of Light. It was said to be hidden in a cave deep in the forest, marked by a special symbol. Elara and Aiden knew their next destination.

They returned to the village and gathered their allies. The Harpers, Silvers, Greens, and Rivers all agreed to help them on their quest. Together, they prepared for the journey into the forest.

The forest was dense and dark, but with their allies by their side, they felt more confident. They followed the clues from the book, searching for the symbol that marked the entrance to the cave.

After hours of searching, they finally found the symbol etched into the side of a large rock. The symbol matched the one described in the book. They carefully examined the rock and found a hidden entrance leading into the cave.

The cave was cold and damp, with water dripping from the walls. They used torches to light their way, and the flickering flames cast strange shadows on the cave walls. The path twisted and turned, leading them deeper into the darkness.

After a long and tiring journey, they reached a large chamber. In the center of the chamber was a pedestal, and on it rested a glowing gem—the Heart of Light. The gem radiated a brilliant light, illuminating the entire chamber.

"This is it," Elara said, her voice filled with awe. "We found the Heart of Light."

Aiden approached the pedestal, carefully lifting the gem. The light from the Heart of Light seemed to push back the darkness in the cave. They could feel its warmth and power.

As they prepared to leave the cave, they heard a noise behind them. The shadowy figures from before appeared, their eyes glowing with anger. They had followed them into the cave.

Elara and Aiden fought bravely, using their skills and the power of the Heart of Light to fend off the shadows. The Heart of Light's glow pushed the shadows back, giving them the advantage.

With a final push, they defeated the shadowy figures and made their way out of the cave. They emerged into the forest, the Heart of Light safely in their possession.

The journey back to the village was filled with relief and hope. They had found the Heart of Light and protected it from the dark forces. The village welcomed them with cheers and celebration.

Elara and Aiden knew that their quest was far from over. The sorcerer was still a threat, and they had to continue protecting their home. But with the Heart of Light and the support of their allies, they felt ready to face whatever challenges lay ahead.

As they looked out over the village, Elara felt a sense of determination. They had made great strides, but the journey was just beginning. Together, they would unravel the mysteries and safeguard their home from the darkness that threatened to engulf it.

The Cursed Glade

Elara and Aiden arrived back at the village with the Heart of Light safely in their possession. The villagers greeted them with cheers and relief, but the sense of danger still lingered. Everyone knew the sorcerer would not give up easily.

The next morning, the elder called a meeting in the village square. Elara, Aiden, and their allies gathered around her, eager to hear what she had to say.

"We have made progress," the elder began. "But there are still many dangers ahead. I have learned of a place that might hold more answers. It is called the Cursed Glade. It is said to be a place of great power and great danger."

Elara and Aiden exchanged worried glances. "What do we need to know about this glade?" Aiden asked.

"The Cursed Glade is an ancient site, hidden deep in the forest," the elder explained. "It is said to be cursed, and many who enter do not return. However, it is also believed to hold secrets that might help us understand and defeat the sorcerer."

The decision was clear. They needed to go to the Cursed Glade. Elara and Aiden prepared for the journey, gathering supplies and making sure they were ready for whatever lay ahead. They set out with their allies, determined to uncover the secrets of the glade.

The path through the forest was thick with underbrush, and the air grew colder as they ventured deeper. The forest seemed to close in around them, and the light from the sun barely reached the ground.

As they walked, they noticed strange markings on the trees—symbols they hadn't seen before. Elara stopped to examine them. "These symbols are not from our village. They must be old and tied to the curse."

Aiden nodded. "We need to be careful. If the glade is cursed, these symbols might be warnings or traps."

They continued cautiously, their senses on high alert. The forest grew darker, and an uneasy silence fell over the group. The usual sounds of the forest—birds chirping, leaves rustling—had vanished. Only their footsteps and the occasional creak of the trees broke the silence.

After hours of walking, they finally reached a clearing. The Cursed Glade lay before them, a vast area filled with twisted trees and dark, tangled vines. The ground was covered in thick fog that swirled around their feet.

"This place feels wrong," Elara said, her voice low. "It's like something is watching us."

The group stepped carefully into the glade. The fog made it difficult to see far, and the trees seemed to shift and move as they walked. The air was thick with a strange energy that made their skin tingle.

In the center of the glade stood a large, ancient tree. Its branches were gnarled and twisted, and its roots seemed to reach deep into the ground. At the base of the tree was a stone altar, covered in moss and vines.

"This must be the place the elder mentioned," Aiden said, looking at the altar. "We should search around it."

They carefully approached the altar, their eyes scanning the area for any clues or signs of danger. As they examined the altar, they noticed strange symbols carved into the stone. The symbols seemed to glow faintly, casting an eerie light.

Elara reached out to touch the symbols, but as her fingers brushed the stone, a sudden gust of wind swept through the glade. The fog swirled violently, and the temperature dropped sharply.

"We need to move!" Aiden shouted, grabbing Elara's arm. "Something's happening!"

The ground beneath them began to shake, and the fog thickened, obscuring their vision. Shadowy figures began to emerge from the fog, their forms shifting and changing. The figures moved closer, their eyes glowing with an ominous light.

Elara and Aiden drew their weapons, ready to defend themselves. The shadowy figures were hostile, their movements quick and erratic. The group fought bravely, using their skills and the power of the Heart of Light to push back the shadows.

Despite their efforts, the shadows seemed endless. Each time they pushed one back, another seemed to appear. The fog made it difficult to see, and the ground continued to shake, adding to their confusion.

"We need to find the source of the curse!" Elara shouted, trying to be heard over the chaos. "There must be something that controls these shadows!"

Aiden nodded, his face determined. "Let's focus on the altar. It might be the key."

They fought their way to the altar, trying to protect themselves from the attacking shadows. The symbols on the altar glowed brighter as they approached, their light piercing through the fog. Elara and Aiden examined the symbols closely, trying to decipher their meaning.

As they studied the symbols, Elara noticed a pattern. The symbols seemed to form a sequence, and she realized that they might be part of a puzzle. "I think we need to solve this puzzle to stop the curse!"

Aiden looked at the symbols and began to arrange them according to the pattern Elara had discovered. The symbols started to glow even brighter, and the shadows seemed to hesitate.

With each correct arrangement, the fog began to clear, and the shadows retreated. The ground stopped shaking, and the eerie energy in the air began to dissipate. The light from the symbols grew stronger, pushing back the darkness.

Finally, the puzzle was complete, and the symbols on the altar shone with a brilliant light. The shadows vanished, and the fog lifted, revealing the true beauty of the glade. The ancient tree stood tall, its branches reaching up to the sky.

Elara and Aiden looked around, their breaths coming in relief. The danger had passed, but they knew that the curse had not been completely broken. There were still secrets to uncover and challenges to face.

They carefully examined the altar and the tree, searching for any additional clues. The symbols on the altar had stopped glowing, and the glade seemed to be at peace. They found a small compartment hidden in the base of the altar, containing an old scroll.

Elara carefully unrolled the scroll and began to read. The scroll contained ancient writings about the history of the Cursed Glade and the dark force that had once controlled it. It spoke of a powerful artifact that had been hidden away to protect against the curse.

"The artifact must be nearby," Aiden said, reading over Elara's shoulder. "It could be the key to breaking the curse completely."

They continued to search the glade, following the clues from the scroll. After some time, they found a hidden entrance beneath the ancient tree. The entrance led to a small chamber filled with ancient relics and magical artifacts.

In the center of the chamber was a pedestal, and on it rested a beautifully crafted amulet. The amulet radiated a soft, golden light, and its design matched the symbols they had seen earlier.

"This must be the artifact from the scroll," Elara said, reaching out to take the amulet. "It could help us defeat the sorcerer and break the curse."

As she picked up the amulet, a wave of energy surged through the chamber. The amulet glowed brightly, and the air filled with a soothing warmth. The curse that had once plagued the glade seemed to be lifting.

Elara and Aiden carefully made their way out of the chamber, the amulet safely in their possession. The glade was calm and serene, and the shadows had vanished completely.

As they returned to the village, they felt a sense of accomplishment. They had faced great danger and uncovered powerful secrets. The Heart of Light and the amulet were important tools in their fight against the sorcerer.

The village celebrated their return, and Elara and Aiden shared the news of their discoveries. The villagers were relieved and grateful, and they prepared for the next steps in their quest to protect their home.

Elara and Aiden knew that their journey was far from over. The sorcerer was still a threat, and they needed to continue their efforts to safeguard the village. But with the power of the Heart of Light and the amulet, they felt ready to face whatever challenges lay ahead.

The Cursed Glade had been a place of great danger, but it had also provided them with valuable tools and knowledge. As they looked out over the village, Elara and Aiden felt a renewed sense of hope and determination.

Their adventure was far from finished, and the road ahead would be filled with challenges. But with their allies by their side and the power of the artifacts, they were prepared to confront the darkness and protect their home from the forces that threatened to engulf it.

The Sorcerer's Lair

Elara and Aiden had returned to the village with the powerful amulet and the Heart of Light. The villagers were hopeful, but everyone knew that their true challenge was still ahead. The sorcerer was out there, and they needed to find his lair to stop him once and for all.

They spent the next few days preparing for the next part of their journey. They gathered their allies and shared what they had learned about the sorcerer and his possible location. The villagers provided supplies and maps, and everyone agreed to help in any way they could.

One night, as Elara and Aiden sat by the fire, they studied an old map they had found. The map showed the land around the village and marked a spot deep in the mountains where the sorcerer's lair might be hidden. The mountains were treacherous and known for their dangerous terrain.

"We need to be careful," Aiden said, tracing the route on the map. "The sorcerer's lair could be well-protected."

Elara nodded. "We should gather as much information as we can. If we can find out more about the sorcerer's defenses, we'll be better prepared."

They set out early the next morning, heading toward the mountains. The path was steep and rocky, and the weather grew colder as they climbed higher. The trees thinned out, and the landscape became more barren. Snow began to fall, adding to the challenge of the journey.

After a few days of hard travel, they reached a narrow pass between two large peaks. The pass was covered in snow, and the wind howled through the mountains. The map indicated that the sorcerer's lair was somewhere beyond this pass.

As they carefully made their way through the pass, they noticed strange markings on the rocks—symbols similar to those they had seen in the Cursed Glade. These markings seemed to glow faintly in the dim light.

"This must be a warning," Elara said, examining the symbols. "We should proceed with caution."

The pass twisted and turned, and the snow made it difficult to see. They followed the markings on the rocks, which led them to a hidden entrance in the side of a mountain. The entrance was a dark, narrow tunnel, partially obscured by snow and ice.

"This must be it," Aiden said, peering into the tunnel. "The sorcerer's lair is likely inside."

They entered the tunnel, their footsteps echoing softly in the darkness. The tunnel was cold and damp, and the walls were covered in a thick layer of ice. They used torches to light their way, the flames casting flickering shadows on the walls.

As they moved deeper into the tunnel, they began to hear strange noises—whispers and faint sounds that seemed to come from all directions. The air grew colder, and the ice on the walls seemed to grow thicker.

"This place feels unsettling," Elara said, her voice barely above a whisper. "It's as if something is watching us."

Aiden nodded. "We need to stay alert. There could be traps or other dangers."

They continued through the tunnel, navigating the icy terrain and avoiding hidden pitfalls. The path twisted and turned, leading them deeper into the mountain. The whispers grew louder, and the air seemed to vibrate with a strange energy.

Finally, they reached a large chamber. The chamber was filled with ancient artifacts and magical items, some of which glowed with an eerie light. In the center of the chamber stood a massive, dark stone throne, and sitting on the throne was the sorcerer.

The sorcerer was a tall figure clad in dark robes, his face obscured by a hood. He exuded a powerful aura, and his eyes glowed with an ominous light. The room was filled with an oppressive darkness, and the temperature seemed to drop even further.

"You finally arrived," the sorcerer said, his voice echoing through the chamber. "I've been expecting you."

Elara and Aiden drew their weapons, ready for battle. "We're here to stop you," Aiden said, his voice steady. "Your reign of terror ends now."

The sorcerer raised his hand, and dark energy crackled around him. "You think you can defeat me so easily? This lair is protected by powerful magic, and you are not prepared for what lies ahead."

With a wave of his hand, the sorcerer summoned dark creatures from the shadows. The creatures were twisted and monstrous, their forms shifting and changing. They moved toward Elara and Aiden, their eyes glowing with a malevolent light.

Elara and Aiden fought bravely, using their skills and the power of the Heart of Light to push back the dark creatures. The creatures were powerful and relentless, but the Heart of Light's glow provided them with strength and protection.

The battle raged on, and the chamber was filled with the sounds of clashing weapons and magical energy. Elara and Aiden managed to defeat the dark creatures one by one, but the sorcerer remained seated on his throne, watching them with a cold, calculating gaze.

As they fought, Elara noticed that the sorcerer was drawing energy from the artifacts around him. The artifacts seemed to be fueling his power, and the chamber was filled with an oppressive darkness.

"We need to stop him from using those artifacts!" Elara shouted to Aiden. "They're giving him strength!"

Aiden nodded and made his way toward the artifacts, using the Heart of Light to push back the darkness. Elara continued to fight the sorcerer's minions, her heart racing with determination.

The sorcerer's eyes glowed brighter as he drew more energy from the artifacts. He raised his hand, and a massive wave of dark energy surged toward Elara and Aiden. They braced themselves, using the Heart of Light to shield against the attack.

The Heart of Light's glow intensified, pushing back the dark energy and creating a barrier of light. The sorcerer's attack faltered, and he looked visibly frustrated.

"You cannot defeat me!" the sorcerer roared. "I am the master of this realm!"

Elara and Aiden pressed on, their resolve unwavering. They knew that they had to destroy the sorcerer's source of power to defeat him. They fought their way through the chamber, attacking the artifacts and breaking the magical connections that fueled the sorcerer's strength.

With each artifact they destroyed, the chamber's darkness lifted, and the sorcerer's power diminished. The sorcerer's rage grew, and he unleashed even more powerful attacks, but Elara and Aiden held their ground.

Finally, they reached the last artifact, a dark crystal embedded in the center of the throne. The crystal pulsed with dark energy, and the sorcerer's power was at its peak. Elara and Aiden worked together to shatter the crystal, their combined strength breaking the dark magic that held it together.

The moment the crystal was destroyed, a wave of light surged through the chamber, dispelling the darkness and weakening the sorcerer. The sorcerer roared in anger, but his power was fading. He struggled to maintain control, but the destruction of the artifacts had left him vulnerable.

Elara and Aiden seized the opportunity and launched their final attack. With a powerful strike, they defeated the sorcerer, and he collapsed to the ground. The dark energy that had surrounded him dissipated, leaving the chamber in a state of calm.

Breathing heavily, Elara and Aiden looked around the chamber. The artifacts were broken, and the oppressive darkness had lifted. The sorcerer's lair was now quiet and serene, a stark contrast to the chaos that had filled it moments before.

"We did it," Aiden said, his voice filled with relief. "The sorcerer is defeated, and his power is broken."

Elara nodded, her eyes reflecting a mix of exhaustion and satisfaction. "It's over. We've stopped him."

They carefully made their way out of the lair, leaving behind the dark chamber and the sorcerer's once-feared domain. The journey back to the village was filled with a sense of accomplishment. They had faced great danger and emerged victorious.

As they arrived in the village, they were greeted with cheers and celebration. The villagers were overjoyed to hear of their success and grateful for their bravery.

Elara and Aiden knew that their journey had been long and challenging, but they had achieved what they set out to do. The village was safe once again, and the threat of the sorcerer had been vanquished.

As they looked out over the village, Elara and Aiden felt a deep sense of fulfillment. They had faced the darkness and emerged stronger, their bond forged through their shared struggles and victories.

The adventure was over, but their story was just beginning. With the village safe and the darkness defeated, they looked forward to the future with hope and determination, ready to embrace whatever challenges lay ahead.

The Hidden w

Elara and Aiden had returned to the village, triumphant but weary from their fight against the sorcerer. The village was celebrating their victory, but Elara couldn't shake the feeling that there was more to uncover. The amulet they had found in the Cursed Glade was still glowing softly, hinting at secrets yet to be revealed.

As the celebration continued, Elara and Aiden took some time to examine the amulet closely. It was intricately designed, with delicate patterns that seemed to change when viewed from different angles. Elara wondered if it held more power or knowledge that could help them understand their next steps.

In the quiet of the night, Elara and Aiden sat by the fire in their tent, studying the amulet. The flames flickered, casting shadows on the walls, and the village's sounds of celebration were a distant murmur.

"There must be something more to this amulet," Elara said, holding it up to the light. "Maybe it's a key to something we don't yet understand."

Aiden nodded, examining the amulet with a thoughtful expression. "We should try to find out more about its history. If it's linked to the sorcerer's power, it could hold important clues."

The next day, Elara and Aiden decided to visit the village's elder to see if she could provide any additional information. The elder was in her study, surrounded by ancient books and scrolls. She looked up with a warm smile as they entered.

"Good to see you both," the elder said. "How can I help you today?"

Elara explained their thoughts about the amulet and their need to learn more about it. The elder nodded and took the amulet, studying it carefully.

"This is a powerful artifact," the elder said after a moment. "It is said to be a key to an ancient hidden chamber. Legends speak of a place filled with great knowledge and magical artifacts."

Elara's eyes widened with interest. "Do you know where this chamber might be?"

The elder nodded. "There are old texts that mention the chamber. It is said to be hidden deep beneath the mountains, in a place that is difficult to find. The amulet might be able to reveal the entrance."

Elara and Aiden were eager to find the hidden chamber. The elder provided them with a few ancient texts and maps that might help in their search. They carefully studied the maps and texts, trying to decipher the clues about the chamber's location.

According to the texts, the hidden chamber could be reached through a series of tunnels and caves that were said to be protected by powerful magic. The amulet was believed to be the key to opening the entrance to these tunnels.

Elara and Aiden prepared for their journey, gathering supplies and making sure they were ready for the challenges ahead. They set out once again toward the mountains, determined to find the hidden chamber.

The journey through the mountains was tough. The path was steep, and the weather was cold and unpredictable. They followed the clues from the texts, searching for any signs that might lead them to the entrance of the hidden chamber.

After several days of trekking, they reached a remote area where the terrain became more rugged. The snow-covered peaks towered above them, and the air was thin and cold. The maps indicated that they were close to the hidden chamber's location.

As they explored the area, they came across a series of ancient stone pillars covered in strange symbols. The symbols matched those on the amulet, and Elara realized that they might be a clue to finding the entrance.

"We need to figure out these symbols," Elara said, studying the pillars. "They could be part of the puzzle to unlock the entrance."

Aiden nodded, examining the symbols closely. "Let's try to match them with the patterns on the amulet."

They worked together, comparing the symbols on the pillars with those on the amulet. After some effort, they managed to arrange the symbols in a sequence that seemed to fit with the patterns on the amulet.

As they completed the sequence, the ground began to shake, and a hidden door in the mountainside slowly opened. A dark passageway was revealed, leading into the depths of the mountain.

"This must be it," Aiden said, looking at the entrance. "Let's go."

They entered the passageway, their torches lighting the way. The tunnel was narrow and winding, and the air was cold and damp. The walls were covered in ancient runes and carvings, adding to the sense of mystery.

As they moved deeper into the tunnel, they encountered several traps—hidden pits, swinging blades, and magical barriers. They used their wits and the Heart of Light to navigate these dangers, carefully avoiding or disarming each trap.

The tunnel finally opened into a vast underground chamber. The chamber was filled with ancient artifacts, glowing with a soft light. In the center of the chamber stood a large stone pedestal with a book resting on it.

"This is amazing," Elara said, looking around the chamber. "There must be so much knowledge here."

Aiden approached the pedestal and carefully picked up the book. The cover was adorned with intricate designs and symbols that matched those on the amulet. He opened the book and began to read.

The book contained ancient writings and spells related to the sorcerer's magic and the history of the hidden chamber. It spoke of powerful artifacts, magical rituals, and secrets that had been protected for centuries.

"This book might hold the answers we need," Aiden said, his eyes scanning the pages. "It could help us understand how to use the amulet and what other secrets this chamber holds."

As they studied the book, they noticed a hidden compartment in the pedestal. Inside, they found a set of keys and a scroll with more instructions about the chamber.

The scroll explained that the chamber was not only a repository of magical knowledge but also a place of protection. The keys were needed to access different sections of the chamber and unlock its full potential.

Elara and Aiden carefully used the keys to open several hidden doors within the chamber. Each door led to new areas filled with magical artifacts, ancient texts, and mysterious objects.

In one of the rooms, they found a large crystal orb that seemed to contain swirling energy. The orb was connected to a complex mechanism that required a specific sequence of actions to activate.

Following the instructions in the book, Elara and Aiden carefully manipulated the mechanism, and the orb began to glow with a brilliant light. The light revealed hidden passages and secret rooms within the chamber.

They explored these new areas, discovering more about the history of the chamber and the artifacts it held. They found ancient scrolls, magical tools, and powerful relics that had been hidden away for centuries.

One of the most important discoveries was a map detailing the locations of other hidden chambers and magical sites across the land. The map showed connections between the hidden chamber and other places of power, which could be crucial in their fight against any remaining threats.

After hours of exploration, Elara and Aiden gathered the most important artifacts and knowledge from the chamber. They knew they had to return to the village and share their findings.

As they made their way out of the hidden chamber, they felt a deep sense of accomplishment. They had uncovered powerful secrets and gained valuable tools to help protect their home.

The journey back to the village was filled with anticipation. They knew that their discoveries would be vital in their ongoing quest to safeguard their world from dark forces.

When they arrived at the village, they were met with excitement and curiosity. The villagers eagerly gathered to hear about their adventure and the secrets they had uncovered.

Elara and Aiden shared their findings, showing the villagers the artifacts, scrolls, and the map they had discovered. The village elder was especially intrigued by the map and the connections it revealed.

"This is incredible," the elder said, examining the map. "We have much more to learn and many more places to explore. Your discovery will help us understand the magic of our world and protect it from future threats."

Elara and Aiden felt proud of their achievements, knowing that their journey had been worth every challenge. The hidden chamber had provided them with powerful knowledge and tools, and their adventure was far from over.

As they looked out over the village, they knew that they had taken an important step in their quest. With the secrets of the hidden chamber revealed, they were better prepared for whatever challenges lay ahead.

The future was uncertain, but Elara and Aiden faced it with hope and determination. They were ready to continue their journey, protect their home, and uncover more mysteries in their world.

The Enchanted Grove

Elara and Aiden stood on the edge of the village, looking at the mysterious map they had found in the hidden chamber. The map showed several locations marked with symbols, and one of these symbols was near an ancient grove deep in the forest.

"The map suggests that there is something important in that grove," Elara said, pointing to a spot marked with an unusual symbol. "We should check it out."

Aiden nodded, ready for another adventure. "Let's prepare for the journey. We don't know what we might find."

They gathered supplies: food, water, and some tools. Elara also packed the Heart of Light and some of the magical artifacts they had discovered in the hidden chamber. After getting everything ready, they set off toward the forest.

The forest was dense and dark. Tall trees with thick branches blocked most of the sunlight. The air was cool and smelled of damp earth and pine. The path was narrow and winding, making it easy to get lost.

Elara and Aiden followed the map carefully, using a compass to stay on track. They walked for hours, their feet crunching on the fallen leaves and twigs. They listened to the sounds of the forest: birds singing, leaves rustling, and the occasional snap of a twig.

As they walked deeper into the forest, they noticed that the trees seemed to grow closer together. The path became less clear, and the forest grew quieter. It felt as if they were entering a different world.

"There's something strange about this place," Aiden said, looking around. "It feels like the forest is alive."

Elara agreed. "We need to stay alert. We don't know what might be waiting for us."

They continued their journey, the trees growing more ancient and gnarled as they went. The map led them to a clearing, and in the center was an old stone archway covered in moss and vines. The archway had the same symbol they had seen on the map.

"This must be the entrance to the enchanted grove," Elara said, approaching the archway.

Aiden examined the archway carefully. "There's something magical about this place. We should be cautious."

They stepped through the archway and found themselves in a beautiful grove. The trees in this grove were different from those in the rest of the forest. They had shimmering leaves that changed color in the light. Flowers bloomed with vibrant colors, and the air was filled with a sweet fragrance.

In the center of the grove was a large, ancient tree with a hollow trunk. The tree seemed to glow with a soft, golden light. At the base of the tree was a pedestal with a glowing crystal orb.

"This is incredible," Elara said, her eyes wide with wonder. "The crystal orb looks like it could be very important."

Aiden agreed. "Let's approach carefully and see what it does."

They walked toward the pedestal. As they got closer, they noticed that the crystal orb was surrounded by intricate symbols. The symbols matched those on the map and the amulet.

Elara took the Heart of Light from her bag and held it up to the orb. The orb's light brightened and began to pulse in rhythm with the Heart of Light. It seemed like the two objects were connected.

"I think the Heart of Light is meant to interact with the orb," Elara said, holding it steady.

The crystal orb began to spin slowly, and the symbols around it started to glow. The symbols formed a pattern that seemed to be a puzzle. Elara and Aiden worked together to match the symbols on the orb with those on the pedestal.

As they completed the pattern, the ground began to shake gently, and a hidden door appeared in the trunk of the ancient tree. The door was covered in more symbols and had a large keyhole in the center.

"This must be the next step," Aiden said, examining the door. "We need to find the key."

Elara looked around the grove, searching for any clues. She noticed a small, hidden compartment in the base of the pedestal. Inside the compartment was a golden key with the same symbols as those on the door.

"We found the key," Elara said, picking it up. "Let's try it."

She inserted the key into the lock and turned it. The door creaked open, revealing a dark passageway leading into the tree. They took a deep breath and entered the passage.

The passage was narrow and lined with more glowing symbols. The air was cool and filled with the sound of dripping water. The walls seemed to pulse with a faint, magical energy.

As they walked through the passage, they came to a large underground chamber. The chamber was filled with ancient books, magical artifacts, and treasures. In the center of the chamber was a large, ornate chest.

"This is amazing," Aiden said, looking around. "There must be so much knowledge and power here."

Elara approached the chest and carefully opened it. Inside, they found a collection of scrolls, each sealed with a wax emblem. The scrolls were written in an ancient language, but there was one scroll that seemed different.

The scroll had a golden ribbon and was covered in intricate designs. Elara unrolled the scroll and saw that it contained detailed information about the magical artifacts and their uses. It also included a map of hidden locations across the land.

"This scroll is incredible," Elara said, examining it closely. "It has information about other magical places and artifacts."

Aiden took out the map and compared it with the one they had found earlier. "The scroll's map has new locations that we haven't seen before. This could lead us to more powerful artifacts."

They carefully packed the scrolls and other treasures into their bags, knowing that they would need to study them further. As they prepared to leave the chamber, they noticed a hidden door in the back of the room.

The door was covered in strange symbols and had a magical lock. Elara used the Heart of Light to interact with the lock, and the door slowly opened. Inside, they found a small, glowing crystal that radiated a warm, golden light.

"This must be another important artifact," Elara said, holding the crystal. "It could be very powerful."

They carefully took the crystal and added it to their collection. As they left the chamber, they felt a sense of accomplishment. They had uncovered new secrets and gained valuable knowledge that would help them in their quest.

The journey back through the enchanted grove was filled with anticipation. They knew that the discoveries they had made would be crucial in their fight against dark forces. The enchanted grove had provided them with powerful artifacts and important information.

When they arrived back at the village, they were greeted with excitement and curiosity. The villagers gathered around to hear about their adventure and see the treasures they had found.

Elara and Aiden shared their discoveries, showing the villagers the scrolls, artifacts, and the glowing crystal. The village elder was particularly interested in the scroll and the map.

"This is remarkable," the elder said, examining the scroll. "The knowledge you have uncovered will help us understand more about the magic of our world and protect it from future threats."

Elara and Aiden felt proud of their achievements. They had taken another important step in their journey and were ready to continue their quest. The enchanted grove had revealed new secrets and provided them with powerful tools for the challenges ahead.

As they looked out over the village, they knew that their adventure was far from over. With the new knowledge and artifacts they had discovered, they were better prepared to face whatever lay ahead. The future was uncertain, but Elara and Aiden were determined to continue their journey and protect their world from dark forces.

The Shadow's Secret

Elara and Aiden had been busy since their return from the enchanted grove. The village was abuzz with excitement over their discoveries. The scrolls, artifacts, and crystal they had found were being carefully studied by the village's scholars and mages.

One evening, as Elara and Aiden were going through the scrolls they had brought back, they noticed something troubling. One of the scrolls had a strange pattern that didn't match any of the others. The symbols seemed to be moving on their own, shifting and changing.

"This doesn't look normal," Aiden said, pointing to the scroll. "It's as if it's trying to tell us something."

Elara agreed. "Let's show this to the elder. She might know what it means."

They took the scroll to the village elder, who was busy studying the other artifacts. When she saw the moving symbols, her eyes widened with concern.

"This is not just a simple scroll," the elder said. "These symbols are changing because they are part of a magical message. It could be a warning or a clue to something important."

Elara and Aiden listened carefully as the elder continued. "There is an old legend about a hidden realm that exists outside our world. This realm is protected by powerful magic and only reveals itself when certain conditions are met."

The elder paused, looking thoughtful. "The scroll might be pointing us to this hidden realm. If the symbols are changing, it could mean that something is trying to reach us or warn us."

Elara and Aiden felt a shiver of excitement and worry. If there was a hidden realm, it could hold important secrets or dangers. They knew they had to investigate.

The elder provided them with a few more ancient texts and maps that might help them find the hidden realm. The texts mentioned a place called the Shadow's Secret, a mysterious land that was said to appear only when the stars aligned in a specific way.

"The alignment of the stars might be our key," the elder said. "You'll need to observe the night sky and compare it with the patterns on the scroll."

Elara and Aiden prepared for another journey, this time to uncover the mystery of the Shadow's Secret. They set out one night to find a clear spot where they could see the stars. The sky was filled with stars, and they set up a telescope to observe the patterns.

They carefully compared the star patterns with those on the scroll. The scroll showed a specific alignment that matched the current night sky. It seemed that the Shadow's Secret was about to reveal itself.

As they continued to observe the sky, a strange phenomenon began to occur. A dark shadow appeared on the horizon, moving toward them. The shadow grew larger and seemed to pulse with a dark energy.

"This is it," Aiden said, watching the shadow. "It's like the scroll is guiding us to this place."

The shadow moved closer, and the ground began to tremble. Elara and Aiden followed the shadow as it moved through the forest, leading them to a hidden cave entrance.

The cave was dark and foreboding. They took out their torches and entered cautiously. The cave walls were covered in strange symbols and glowing crystals that cast eerie shadows.

The deeper they went, the more intense the feeling of magic became. The cave seemed to be alive, and the air was thick with an otherworldly energy. They followed the tunnel, which twisted and turned, leading them deeper into the earth.

Eventually, they reached a large chamber with a high ceiling. In the center of the chamber was a massive stone altar, covered in dust and cobwebs. The altar had more of the moving symbols and a large, dark crystal embedded in its center.

"This must be the heart of the Shadow's Secret," Elara said, approaching the altar. "The crystal looks like it's connected to the magic of this place."

Aiden examined the altar and the crystal. "The symbols on the altar match those on the scroll. We might need to interact with the crystal to unlock the secrets of this realm."

Elara carefully touched the dark crystal. As she did, the symbols on the altar began to glow and shift. The chamber was filled with a soft, pulsating light, and the air grew colder.

The dark crystal started to glow brighter, and a hidden door in the chamber wall slowly opened. The door revealed another passageway leading further into the hidden realm.

"We have to go through that door," Aiden said, looking at Elara. "Let's see what's on the other side."

They entered the passageway, which led them to a vast, shadowy landscape. The sky was a swirling mix of dark clouds and strange lights, and the ground was covered in dark, shimmering dust.

In the distance, they saw a large, imposing structure—a dark fortress that seemed to float above the ground. It was surrounded by swirling shadows and had an aura of ancient, dark magic.

"That must be where the secrets of the Shadow's Secret are hidden," Elara said. "We need to find a way inside."

They approached the fortress, using the Heart of Light to illuminate their path. The fortress was surrounded by a magical barrier that pulsed with dark energy.

"We need to find a way to break through this barrier," Aiden said, studying the barrier closely. "There must be a way to dispel it."

Elara looked around and noticed that there were dark symbols carved into the ground around the barrier. They matched the symbols on the scroll and the altar.

"If these symbols are connected to the barrier," Elara said, "maybe we need to interact with them to break through."

They carefully followed the symbols, using the Heart of Light to reveal hidden clues. As they completed the pattern, the barrier began to weaken and flicker.

With a final touch of the Heart of Light, the barrier dissolved, allowing them to enter the fortress. They stepped inside and found themselves in a grand hall with high ceilings and dark, swirling mists.

The hall was filled with ancient artifacts and magical objects, each glowing with a dark, mysterious light. At the end of the hall was a large, ornate throne with a figure sitting on it.

The figure was cloaked in shadows and had an air of power and authority. As Elara and Aiden approached, the figure looked up and revealed a face that was both familiar and strange.

"Welcome," the figure said in a deep, resonant voice. "I have been expecting you."

Elara and Aiden were taken aback. The figure's face was shrouded in shadows, but they could see a pair of piercing eyes that seemed to know everything about them.

"Who are you?" Elara asked, her voice steady despite her nerves. "And what is the Shadow's Secret?"

The figure smiled faintly. "I am the guardian of the Shadow's Secret. This realm holds ancient knowledge and powerful magic that has been hidden away for centuries. It is a place where the boundaries between worlds are thin, and only those who are truly worthy can access its secrets."

The figure stood up from the throne and approached them. "You have proven yourselves worthy by finding your way here and solving the puzzles. Now, you must make a choice."

Elara and Aiden exchanged glances. "What choice?" Aiden asked.

The guardian gestured to a large, ancient book lying on a pedestal. "This book contains the knowledge of the Shadow's Secret. You can take it and learn its secrets, but be aware that with great knowledge comes great responsibility. The power of this realm can change the world, for better or for worse."

Elara and Aiden approached the book, feeling its weight and significance. They knew that whatever they decided would have a profound impact on their quest and the world they were trying to protect.

"We need to understand what we're dealing with," Elara said, looking at Aiden. "This knowledge might be crucial for our fight against the dark forces."

Aiden nodded. "We should take the book and learn from it. But we must use the knowledge wisely and responsibly."

With determination, they took the ancient book from the pedestal. As they did, the fortress began to shift and change, the shadows and mists swirling around them. The guardian's voice echoed through the hall.

"Remember," the guardian said, "the Shadow's Secret is not just about power. It is about balance, responsibility, and the choices you make. Use the knowledge wisely, and you will find the strength to face the challenges ahead."

As Elara and Aiden left the fortress, the realm began to dissolve around them. The dark landscape faded, and they found themselves back in the forest, with the night sky clear and calm.

They looked at the ancient book in their hands, knowing that their journey had brought them to an important turning point. The knowledge they had gained from the Shadow's Secret would guide them in their quest and help them face the dark forces threatening their world.

With a sense of purpose and resolve, Elara and Aiden made their way back to the village. They were ready to continue their journey, armed with the secrets of the Shadow's Secret and determined to protect their world from the forces of darkness.

The Final Confrontation

Elara and Aiden returned to the village with the ancient book from the Shadow's Secret. They were eager to share what they had learned and prepare for the challenges ahead. The village was busy as usual, but there was an air of anticipation in the air.

As they entered the village square, the villagers gathered around them, curious about their adventure. Elara and Aiden explained their journey and the mysterious realm they had discovered. The villagers listened with wide eyes and hushed whispers.

"The ancient book holds the key to understanding the dark forces we are facing," Elara said, holding up the book. "We must study it and prepare for what lies ahead."

The village elder and the scholars began to examine the book carefully. The pages were filled with ancient symbols and detailed illustrations of magical creatures and powerful spells. It was clear that the knowledge contained in the book was vast and complex.

"We need to decipher the book's contents," the elder said. "It will guide us in our battle against the dark forces threatening our world."

Elara and Aiden spent days studying the book, working with the elder and the scholars. They learned about powerful spells, ancient artifacts, and hidden

THE FINAL CONFRONTATION

strengths. The more they studied, the more they understood the gravity of their mission.

One evening, as they were deep in their studies, a sudden chill filled the air. Elara and Aiden felt a strange presence, and the room grew dark. The village's magical wards were activated, signaling that something was approaching.

The elder, with a worried expression, said, "The dark forces have found us. They are coming for the book."

Elara and Aiden prepared for the impending attack. They gathered their weapons and protective gear, ready to defend the village. The sky outside darkened, and a cold wind blew through the village.

As night fell, a horde of shadowy creatures appeared at the edge of the village. They were twisted, dark forms, with glowing red eyes and menacing growls. The villagers rallied together, ready to fight.

Elara and Aiden took their positions, using the knowledge from the book to set up magical defenses and traps. The villagers used their skills and weapons to fend off the dark creatures. The battle was fierce, with flashes of magic and clashing steel filling the night.

Amid the chaos, Elara and Aiden noticed a figure moving through the shadows. It was cloaked in darkness and seemed to be directing the creatures. They realized that this figure was likely the source of the dark magic.

"We need to stop that figure," Aiden said, pointing to the shadowy figure. "It's controlling the dark creatures."

Elara nodded. "Let's go."

They fought their way through the dark creatures, making their way toward the figure. The battle was intense, with dark magic and powerful spells being exchanged. Elara and Aiden used their knowledge and skills to push forward.

When they finally reached the figure, they saw that it was a tall, dark sorcerer with a commanding presence. His eyes glowed with a sinister light, and he held a staff covered in dark runes.

"You're too late," the sorcerer said with a cruel smile. "The power of the Shadow's Secret belongs to me now."

Elara and Aiden confronted the sorcerer, ready to fight. The sorcerer raised his staff, unleashing a wave of dark energy that pushed them back. They struggled to keep their footing as the dark magic swirled around them.

"This is it," Elara said, her voice steady despite the danger. "We need to use the book's knowledge to defeat him."

Aiden agreed. "Let's find the spell that can counter his magic."

They quickly searched the book, finding a powerful spell designed to counter dark magic. They recited the incantation, channeling the energy of the Heart of Light. The spell created a barrier of light that protected them from the sorcerer's attacks.

The sorcerer was taken aback by the barrier but quickly recovered. He used his staff to cast a powerful spell that shattered the barrier. The battle continued, with both sides using their magic and strength to gain the upper hand.

Elara and Aiden fought bravely, using the spells and techniques they had learned from the book. They managed to weaken the sorcerer, but he was still a formidable opponent. The battle seemed to go on forever, with neither side giving in.

THE FINAL CONFRONTATION

At a crucial moment, Elara remembered a piece of information from the book. It mentioned a way to neutralize the sorcerer's dark magic by using the Heart of Light in a specific way.

"We need to focus the Heart of Light's energy into a single, powerful beam," Elara said to Aiden. "It might be able to break through his defenses."

Aiden nodded, and they quickly prepared the Heart of Light. They concentrated its energy, focusing it into a single, bright beam. The beam shot toward the sorcerer, piercing through his dark magic and striking him directly.

The sorcerer screamed in pain as the light overwhelmed him. The dark creatures he had controlled began to retreat, their dark forms dissolving into shadows. The sorcerer fell to the ground, his power broken.

With the sorcerer defeated, the remaining dark creatures vanished, and the night returned to calm. The villagers cheered, relieved that the threat had been vanquished.

Elara and Aiden, exhausted but victorious, returned to the village. The elder and the villagers congratulated them on their bravery and thanked them for saving the village.

"We couldn't have done it without the book and the Heart of Light," Elara said, looking at the ancient book. "The knowledge we gained was crucial in our battle."

The elder nodded. "You have done well. The village is safe once again, and the dark forces have been driven away."

As dawn approached, Elara and Aiden looked out at the village. The battle had been hard-fought, but they had succeeded in protecting their home. The knowledge from the Shadow's Secret had proven to be a powerful tool in their fight against darkness.

"We've accomplished a lot," Aiden said, looking at Elara. "But there will always be more challenges ahead."

Elara smiled, her resolve stronger than ever. "We'll face them together. As long as we have each other and the knowledge we've gained, we can overcome any obstacle."

With a sense of accomplishment and hope for the future, Elara and Aiden prepared for the next chapter of their journey. They knew that the path ahead would be filled with more mysteries and adventures, but they were ready to face whatever came their way.

The Dawn of a New Era

The village of Eldoria was finally at peace. After the battle against the dark sorcerer and his shadowy minions, life slowly returned to normal. The villagers, grateful and relieved, celebrated their heroes, Elara and Aiden. They held a grand feast in their honor, and stories of their bravery became a part of the village's rich history.

Elara and Aiden, though exhausted from their recent trials, found solace in the simple joys of village life. The Heart of Light, now a symbol of their victory, was placed in a special chamber within the village's Hall of Records. The ancient book, too, was kept safely under the watchful eyes of the village scholars, its secrets now a source of knowledge and strength for future generations.

In the months that followed, Elara and Aiden continued their studies and worked to strengthen the village's defenses. They trained the villagers in the use of magic and combat, ensuring that they were prepared for any future threats. Their bond grew stronger as they faced each challenge together, each adventure deepening their understanding of the world and their place in it.

One crisp autumn day, as the leaves turned gold and crimson, Elara and Aiden walked through the village, reflecting on their journey. They had come a long way since they first discovered the ancient book and ventured into the shadowy realm. Their lives had changed forever, and they had grown in ways they had never imagined.

As they strolled through the marketplace, they were greeted by friendly faces and warm smiles. The village was thriving, its people united and hopeful. Elara and Aiden knew that their efforts had made a lasting impact, and they took pride in the knowledge that they had played a crucial role in protecting their home.

One evening, the village elder gathered everyone for a special ceremony. The people of Eldoria, along with Elara and Aiden, gathered around the central square, where a new monument had been erected. It was a beautifully carved statue of a knight and a mage, symbolizing bravery, unity, and the strength of their community.

The elder spoke to the crowd, her voice filled with pride and gratitude. "Today, we celebrate not only our victory but also the spirit of courage and determination that brought us through the darkest of times. Elara and Aiden have shown us that even in the face of great danger, hope and bravery can light the way."

As the ceremony concluded, Elara and Aiden stood together, their hearts full of joy and contentment. They had faced many trials and challenges, but they had emerged stronger and more united. Their journey had not only saved their village but had also forged a deep and lasting bond between them.

With the dark forces defeated and the village safe, Elara and Aiden looked forward to a future filled with new adventures and opportunities. They knew that their work was far from over, but they were ready to face whatever came next with the same courage and determination that had seen them through their previous trials.

As the sun set over the horizon, casting a warm glow over the village, Elara and Aiden stood side by side, ready to embrace the new dawn of their lives. The world was full of mysteries and challenges, but they were prepared to face them together, knowing that as long as they had each other, they could overcome anything.

Their journey had taught them that true strength lay not only in magic and power but in the bonds they forged and the hope they carried in their hearts. And with that hope, they looked forward to a future filled with promise, knowing that their story was just beginning.

The adventure of Elara and Aiden had come to a close, but the lessons they learned and the impact they made would be remembered for generations. Their bravery, wisdom, and unity had turned the tide against darkness and brought hope to their world.

The village of Eldoria thrived, its people inspired by the courage of their heroes. Elara and Aiden continued to protect and guide their community, using their knowledge and experience to ensure that the peace they had fought so hard for would endure.

As time went on, stories of their deeds spread far and wide, becoming legends told around fires and passed down through generations. Their names became synonymous with hope and heroism, and their legacy lived on in the hearts of those they had saved.

The Heart of Light and the ancient book remained symbols of their triumph, reminding all who saw them of the power of knowledge, courage, and friendship. Elara and Aiden's journey had taught them that even in the face of the darkest shadows, there was always a light to guide the way.

And so, as the seasons changed and new adventures awaited, Elara and Aiden continued to embrace the unknown, knowing that their story was a testament to the enduring strength of the human spirit and the unbreakable bonds that united them. Their tale was one of mystery, adventure, and ultimate triumph—a reminder that even the greatest challenges could be overcome with courage, unity, and a steadfast heart.

www.ingramcontent.com/pod-product-compliance
Lightning Source LLC
LaVergne TN
LVHW050026080526
838202LV00069B/6935